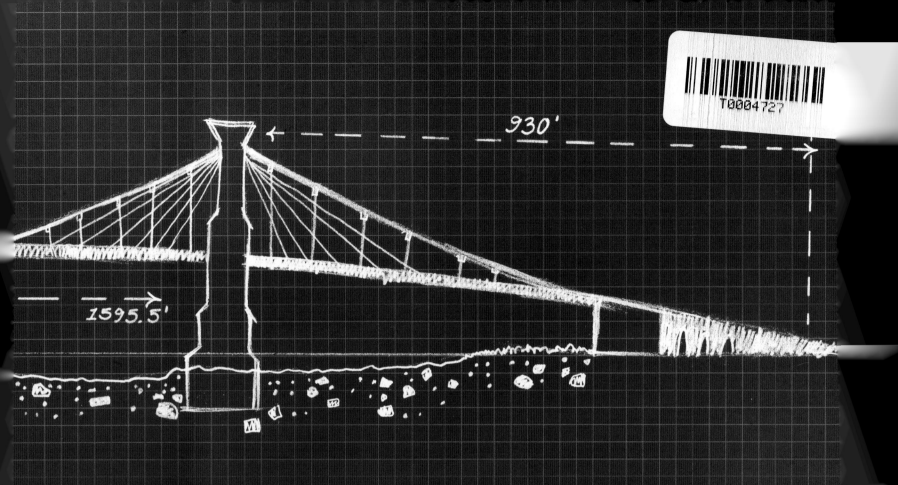

930'

1595.5'

48106-2'

FARRAGUT

For Alyssa, Mom, Meredith, Bub, Laurie, Emily,
and all the strong women in my life

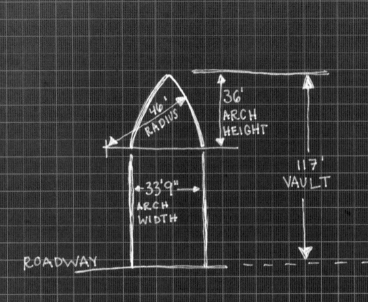

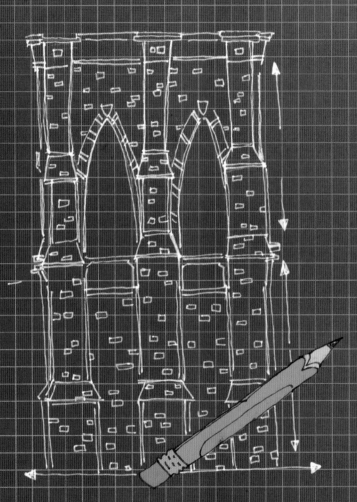

Published by Roaring Brook Press
Roaring Brook Press is a division of Holtzbrinck Publishing Holdings Limited Partnership
175 Fifth Avenue, New York, NY 10010
mackids.com

Library of Congress Control Number: 2018944883
ISBN: 978-1-250-15532-0

Our books may be purchased in bulk for promotional, educational, or business use.
Please contact your local bookseller or the Macmillan Corporate
and Premium Sales Department at (800) 221-7945 ext. 5442
or by e-mail at MacmillanSpecialMarkets@macmillan.com.

First edition, 2019
Book design by Christina Dacanay
Printed in China by Hung Hing Off-set Printing Co. Ltd., Heshan City, Guangdong Province

10 9 8 7 6

SECRET ENGINEER

How Emily Roebling Built
the Brooklyn Bridge

Rachel Dougherty

Roaring Brook Press
New York

Emily Warren was a bright, shiny spark who loved to learn.

Like many girls, she studied sewing and piano. Unlike many girls, she also studied math and science.

In time, she married a spry young engineer named Washington Roebling, whose mind was just as hungry as hers.

The Roebling family built bridges. Washington's father, John A. Roebling, was considered one of the greatest engineers of his time, and now he had a risky new idea.

He told Washington and Emily he had designed a bridge to span the quick, whirling waters of the East River and to finally link Manhattan and Brooklyn. He planned to build two colossal towers and sling a 14,000-foot web of steel cable between them to create the grandest avenue the world had ever seen.

John wanted to send his son to Europe to learn about a new technology for building bridges.

Emily insisted that she would accompany him.

In Europe, Emily and Washington explored historic towns, tasted new foods, and studied the most recent advance in bridge building: the caisson.

2. WAGONS MOVE MUD AND ROCKS FROM THE RIVERBED TO A BARGE.

1. WORKERS IN THE CAISSON BREAK BOULDERS AND SHOVEL MUD, DIGGING DEEPER TOWARD THE SOLID RIVER BOTTOM.

A caisson is like a giant, open box turned upside down and sunk into the water. The opening at the bottom traps air as the box sinks, so it's dry inside. This allows workers to dig deep into the riverbed to find solid rock to build upon. These caissons, once fixed to the firm bedrock, form a sturdy base for the bridge's towers—strong enough to support the structure's weight.

Emily and Washington hurried back to New York, buzzing with discovery.

John wove two caissons into his design and prepared to build the great bridge. But he died before construction began in 1870. Washington would have to take over as chief engineer.

The caissons were larger than any ever made. The base of each one measured about 17,000 square feet. Just building them seemed nearly impossible, and that was only the beginning.

1.

WORKERS BUILD THE CAISSON ON DRY LAND.

2.

THEN THEY CAREFULLY FLOAT THE AIRTIGHT CONTAINER OUT ONTO THE RIVER.

3.
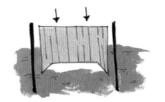
ONCE THE CAISSON IS IN PLACE, WORKERS SINK IT, DISPLACING THE SURROUNDING WATER AND TRAPPING AIR INSIDE.

4.

WHEN IT REACHES THE RIVER BOTTOM, WORKERS CAN DESCEND AND START DIGGING.

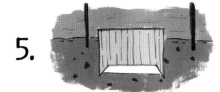

5. AS THE WORKERS DIG, THE CAISSON DROPS.

6. EVENTUALLY, THEY DIG PAST THE SOFT RIVERBED AND REACH SOLID ROCK.

7. WORKERS THEN FILL THE CAISSON WITH CONCRETE AND BUILD THE BRIDGE'S TOWER ON TOP.

Washington soon discovered that construction inside the caissons was muddy, dark, and sweltering. After hours in the caisson every day, he returned home aching and dizzy, but he pressed on. Washington drew plans late into the night, with Emily by his side.

Emily heard that some of the workers were falling ill with pain, weakness, and nausea. They called it "caisson sickness." Then, in 1872, Washington—like many of his workers—collapsed on the dock, and he had to be ferried back home to Brooklyn.

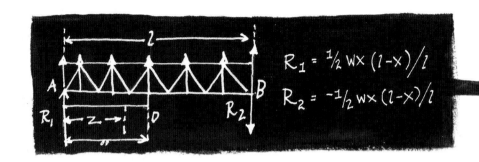

$$R_1 = \tfrac{1}{2} \, wx \, (l-x)/l$$

$$R_2 = -\tfrac{1}{2} \, wx \, (l-x)/l$$

Weeks later, Washington still couldn't get out of bed.
Emily insisted she'd be his eyes and ears.

And legs.

And arms.

As Washington's eyesight dimmed from the caisson sickness, he dictated instructional letters to Emily, and she read construction reports to him. Washington could breathe a little easier knowing Emily would be at the work site.

But Washington's words felt clunky and confusing when Emily repeated them to the engineers. She faithfully copied the terms and equations, but they seemed like a foreign language.

She was nervous. Construction on the bridge was only just beginning, and there was so much she didn't know.

So Emily started to read. She studied bridge engineering, and learned
from Washington and the assistant engineers.

As she studied, the mechanics of the bridge became clearer.

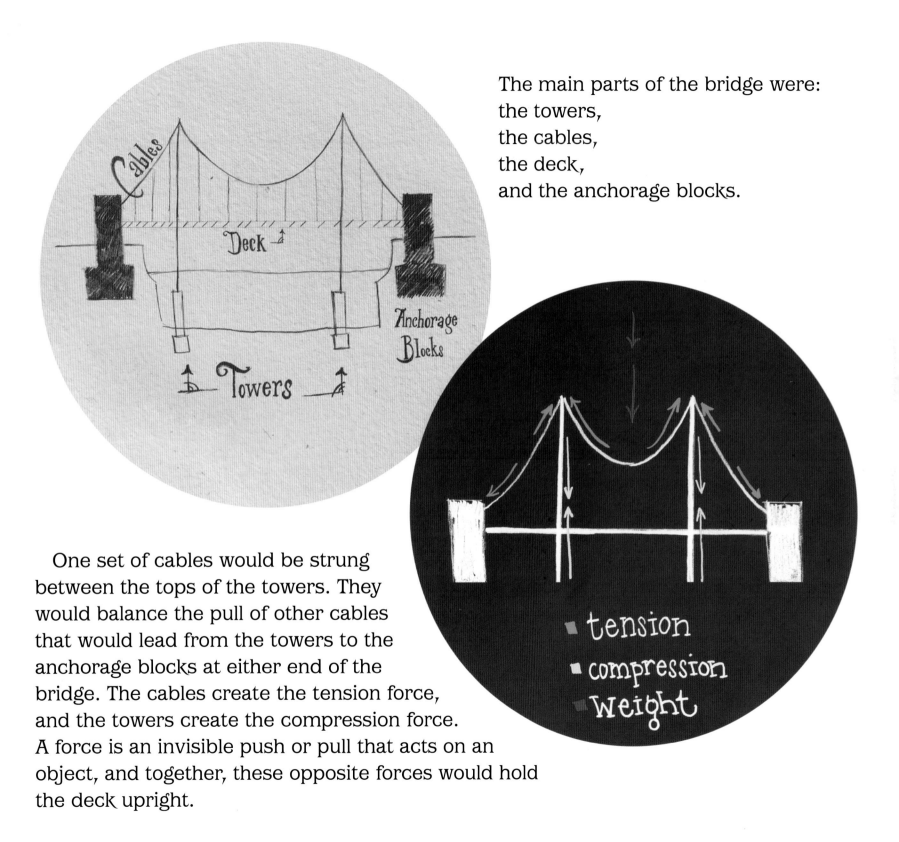

The main parts of the bridge were:
the towers,
the cables,
the deck,
and the anchorage blocks.

Cables

Deck

Anchorage
Blocks

Towers

- tension
- compression
- weight

One set of cables would be strung between the tops of the towers. They would balance the pull of other cables that would lead from the towers to the anchorage blocks at either end of the bridge. The cables create the tension force, and the towers create the compression force. A force is an invisible push or pull that acts on an object, and together, these opposite forces would hold the deck upright.

catenary

The more Emily learned, the more confident she felt.

As time went on, she could see the drawings coming to life.

She saw the steel cables swooping between the towers in what she'd learned was called a catenary curve— the perfect natural arc of a cable held only at its ends, like a clothesline or a jump rope.

She saw the tiny ink scratches she'd squinted at on paper transform into huge vertical cables called suspenders, which would shift the weight of the bridge deck to the main cables. She grinned, knowing that each suspender could hold seventy tons.

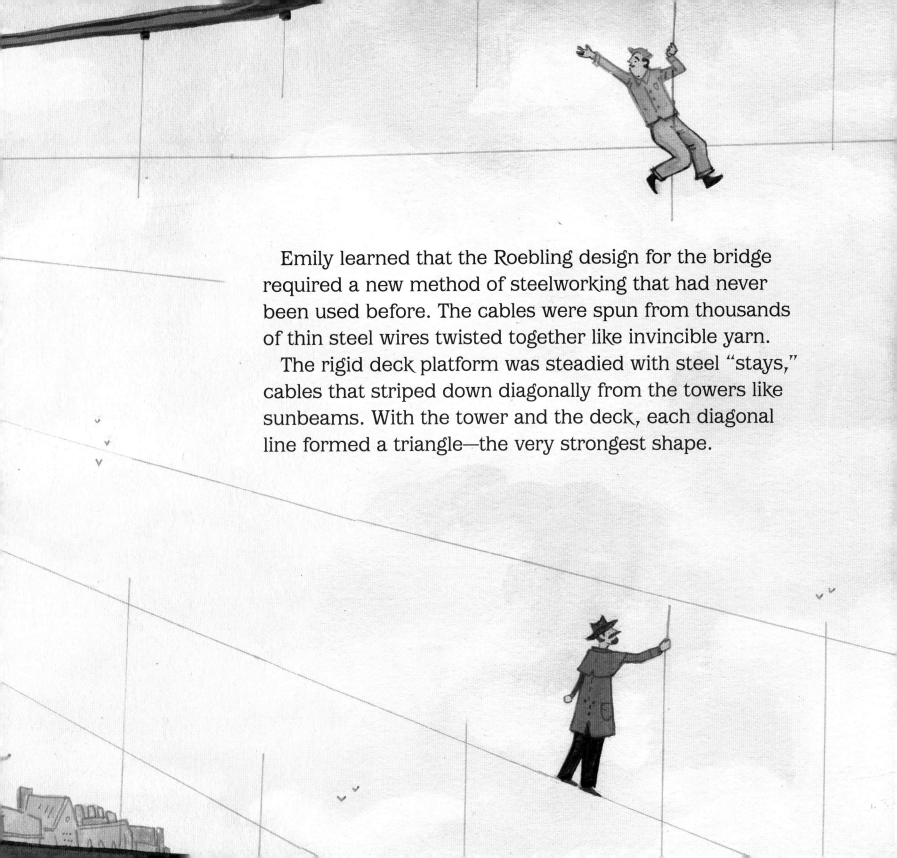

Emily learned that the Roebling design for the bridge required a new method of steelworking that had never been used before. The cables were spun from thousands of thin steel wires twisted together like invincible yarn.

The rigid deck platform was steadied with steel "stays," cables that striped down diagonally from the towers like sunbeams. With the tower and the deck, each diagonal line formed a triangle—the very strongest shape.

No steel mill had ever been asked to make steel cables like these before, and the manufacturers wanted to meet with Washington to make sure they understood the plans. But Washington fretted—if word got out about how sick he was, and that a woman was in charge, the project would surely be taken away from the Roeblings, despite all their work.

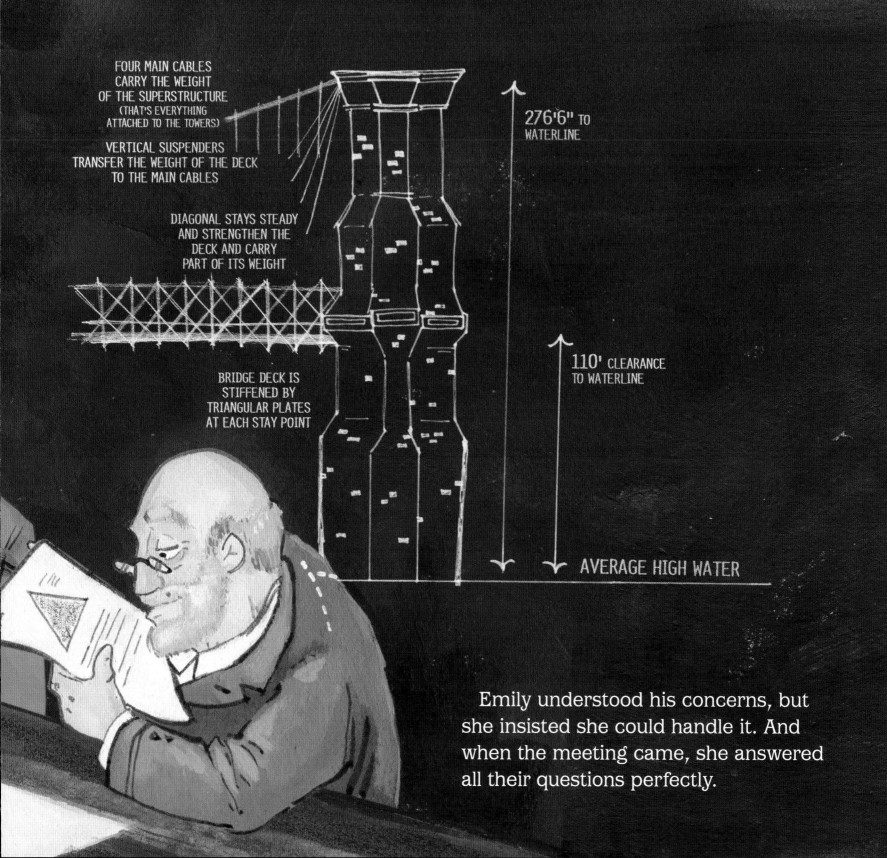

Emily understood his concerns, but she insisted she could handle it. And when the meeting came, she answered all their questions perfectly.

More than ten years had passed since Emily had taken the reins, and the bridge was nearly built. She saw the main cables stretching across the wide river. From her window they looked as delicate as spider silk, but she thought proudly of the equations she'd studied to calculate the cables' strength.

But just before the bridge was set to open, the public, who had never seen a bridge this large, began to worry.

The skinny wires look too weak, they said.
The river is too wide, they said.
Everyone will fall into the water and drown!

Emily insisted they were wrong.

She trusted the thickness and strength of the steel cables, the stability of the diagonal stays, and the balance of the anchorage blocks against the towers. She knew the equations by heart.

A week before the grand opening, Emily rode in an open carriage on the first trip across the finished bridge. She carried a rooster in her lap as a symbol of victory.

When the Brooklyn Bridge opened on May 24, 1883, the two cities set off rockets and fireworks. Bands played from steamboats below all night long. Crowds gathered on both riverbanks, and on boats in between, to celebrate the great feat of engineering—never even knowing about the contributions of an insistent woman named Emily Roebling.

Author's Note

As a child, I was a stream of questions. Why do crabs walk sideways, how do kites stay up, who makes traffic lights? My parents filled my bookshelves with encyclopedias and biographies, and I fell in love with the real men and women of history who answered my questions. Some biographies began so impressively that I'd know right from the first page that the subject was special. But my favorites have always been the underdogs—the ones who have greatness dropped in their laps. That's how I came to love Emily Roebling.

More About Emily

Emily Warren was born on September 23, 1843, the second youngest of twelve children. Her brother Gouverneur Kemble Warren, thirteen years older than Emily, recognized her talents for science and arithmetic at an early age, and enrolled her in secondary school when she was fifteen. In the 1850s, girls rarely pursued education beyond what they learned from childhood governesses. But Emily attended a school offering courses in history and science, in addition to "traditional female pursuits."

Gouverneur introduced Emily to Washington Roebling, with whom he had served during the Civil War. Shortly after Emily and Washington's wedding, Washington's father sent him to Ohio to work on a bridge. Thinking Emily would only visit occasionally, Washington made his living arrangements without her. But Emily insisted on joining him. Despite some opposition from his father, Washington yielded and brought her along.

Two years later, John Roebling took on the Brooklyn Bridge. Brooklyn was a separate city from New York at the time, and slow, crowded ferries were the only way to cross the East River. John asked Washington to travel to Europe to study pneumatic caissons, which could be pressurized with air and used underwater. Even though she was expecting a child, Emily refused to be left behind. Their only son was born in Germany and named John A. Roebling after his grandfather.

In 1869, while examining a construction site for the Brooklyn Bridge, the elder John A. Roebling injured his foot. Unfortunately, in this time before modern medicine, the injury became infected and proved fatal, leaving Washington to take over the building of the bridge.

After Washington became ill with caisson sickness in 1872, Emily kept the project afloat. When challenged by the trustees of the bridge, she fought to keep them from removing Washington from his post as chief engineer. When the steel manufacturers had questions, Emily advised them. When the public clamored about the safety of the bridge, Emily arranged lectures given by a master mechanic to calm their fears. It is now rumored that she even wrote his presentations.

Once the great bridge was completed, Emily and Washington lived in Troy, New York, for four years. Then they returned to their home in Trenton, New Jersey. Washington's health improved somewhat, and he continued operating the family wire business. But Emily did not stop learning. She went on to earn a law degree at New York University. Her final essay was entitled "A Wife's Disabilities," and in it she pleaded for the law to treat men and women equally. She passed away in 1903 at the age of fifty-nine.

Though Emily was born at a time when women were not given much education or professional opportunity, when life asked more of her, she rose to the occasion. Her mind sharp and her hands steady, Emily proved that women could be as successful in science and engineering as any man.

GLOSSARY

anchorage block: A massive masonry block heavy enough to offset the weight of the bridge. For the Brooklyn Bridge, each one weighs about 60,000 tons.

cable: Thick rope made of many metal wires wrapped together.

caisson sickness: An illness caused by nitrogen bubbles that form in the body when a person moves too quickly from an area with high pressure, such as deep underwater, to an area with lower pressure, such as the water's surface. Called decompression sickness or "the bends" today, it can affect scuba divers.

catenary curve: The natural curve of a hanging rope or chain when held at both ends.

deck: The roadway or walkway of a bridge.

force: An invisible push or pull on an object.

stay: A cable that runs diagonally between a tower and the deck of a bridge.

suspender: A cable that hangs vertically between the main suspension cables and the deck of a bridge.

tower: A structure that supports the cables and the deck of a bridge.

SELECT BIBLIOGRAPHY

Erickson, Margery O. *A Few Citizens of Philipstown*. Garrison, NY: Capriole Press, 1990.

McCullough, David. *The Great Bridge: The Epic Story of the Building of the Brooklyn Bridge*. New York: Simon & Schuster, 1972.

Steinman, D. B. *The Builders of the Bridge: The Story of John Roebling and His Son*. New York: Harcourt, Brace, 1945.

Weigold, Marilyn E. *Silent Builder: Emily Warren Roebling and the Brooklyn Bridge*. Port Washington, NY: Associated Faculty Press, 1984.

FURTHER READING

Cornille, Didier. *Who Built That? Bridges: An Introduction to Ten Great Bridges and Their Designers*. New York: Princeton Architectural Press, 2016.

Curlee, Lynn. *Brooklyn Bridge*. New York: Atheneum Books for Young Readers, 2001.

Jones Prince, April. *Twenty-One Elephants and Still Standing*. Boston: Houghton Mifflin, 2005.

Mann, Elizabeth. *The Brooklyn Bridge: The Story of the World's Most Famous Bridge and the Remarkable Family That Built It*. New York: Mikaya Press, 2006.

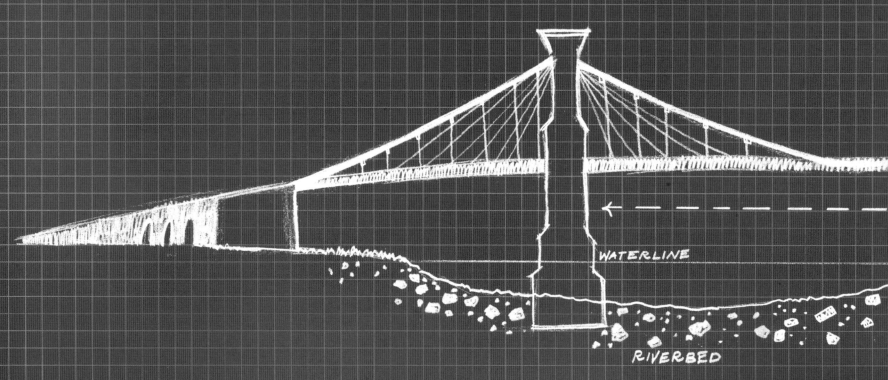

WATERLINE

RIVERBED